Shhh!

Written by Michèle Dufresne

The Snake Is Sleeping

PIONEER VALLEY EDUCATIONAL PRESS, INC.

There are many kinds of snakes.

Some snakes are small,
and some snakes are big.

Snakes are **reptiles**.

Snakes have scales.

2

Scales help snakes slither across rough ground without getting hurt. The scales also protect them and keep their bodies from drying out.

This snake rests on a rock.

The sun has made the rock hot.

Snakes are **cold-blooded**.

They like to nap in hot spots.

Cold-blooded animals, like snakes, cannot control their body temperature. They need heat from the sun to warm up and shade to cool down.

This snake takes a nap by a lake.

A brave bug lands on the snake.

The snake wakes up.

Oh no! Look out, bug!

Can you see the snake's **fangs**?

Small snakes eat bugs, while larger ones hunt frogs, lizards, and other small animals for food. Some snakes can eat animals up to three times bigger than their heads.

Snip-snap!

What a good snack for the snake!

Snakes shed their skin.

This snake will rub up on a branch.

Then it will **slither** out of its skin.

Unlike human skin that grows continuously, snake skin doesn't stretch. As snakes get larger, at times they must shed their old skin to make room for their increasing size.

A male snake sits

in the shade by a gate.

It wants to find a mate.

A big snake naps in the tall grass.

Who can spot it?

Does the **predator** see it?

Camouflage helps snakes blend into dirt, grass, rocks, or sand, so they are safe while they rest.

The snake wakes up
and shakes its **tail.**

Run away quick, predator!

A snake might shake its tail as a warning
to scare off predators. For example,
a rattlesnake shakes its tail to make a
rattling sound. But even a nonvenomous
snake sometimes mimics this behavior by
shaking its tail against dry leaves or grass.

glossary

cold-blooded: an animal that cannot control its body temperature so it needs the sun to warm up and shade to cool down

fangs: long, sharp, hollow teeth

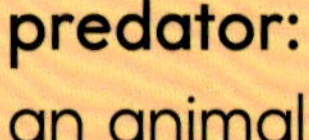

predator: an animal that hunts and eats other animals

reptiles: animals that are cold-blooded, have scales, and usually lay eggs

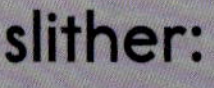

slither: to move smoothly along the ground

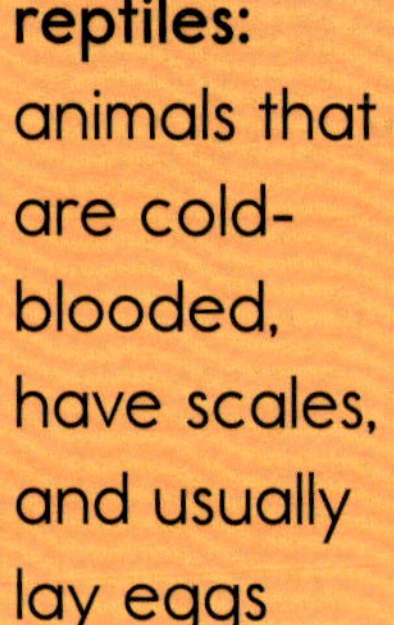

tail: the part of an animal's body that sticks out from its back end